imagination series # 8

A Small Asymmetry

For Susan —
Sister in the art,
and long-time Walter buddy.

Poems by

John Donoghue

at Walter
2006

Cleveland State University Poetry Center

ACKNOWLEDGMENTS

Grateful acknowledgement is made to the editors of the following publications where some of these poems first appeared: *Alaska Quarterly Review*: "Redress." *Marlboro Review:* "In the Meantime," "Waiting for the Muse in Lakeview Cemetery," "Sheila's Auras." *The Four Way Reader #2* edited by Carlen Arnett, Jane Brox, Dzvinia Orlowsky, and Martha Rhodes, and published by Four Way Books: "Images," "One Bedroom, Four Floors Up." *The Lancet*: "Labyrinth." Reprinted with permission from Elsevier (*The Lancet*, 1998, Vol. 352, No. 9121, p. 76). *Poetry East*: "Lackawanna." *Seattle Review*: "Relativity." *The Virginia Quarterly Review*: "Articles of Exploration." *The Western Journal of Medicine*: "Physical." Reprinted with permission from the BMJ Publishing Group (*The Western Journal of Medicine*, 1997, Vol. 167, No. 2, p.114).

A special thanks to the members of the Butcher Shop Workshop in Cleveland for their support and intelligence, and for their toughness when some of these poems were put on the block.

To the many Warren Wilson Alumni Conference participants over the years—I owe you all a huge debt for your advice and encouragement, for showing me how to dress properly, and for being great dancers and a wonderful community of writers.

Thanks to Susan Grimm Dumbrys for her invaluable editorial skills, and to Rita Grabowski for pulling all this together in record time.

Thanks also to Dr. Ron Golovan for inadvertently providing language for the poem "Physical" and for the title of the book.

I am forever indebted to the following poets for the seriousness and intelligence they bring to their work of teaching, and for leading me to a deeper understanding of the importance of writing to this life: Joan Aleshire, Stephen Dobyns, Heather McHugh, Michael Ryan, and Ellen Bryant Voigt.

And thanks to Lewis Buzbee for his support and encouragement.

Excerpt from "Men With Small Heads," from *New and Selected Poems, 1975-1995* by Thomas Lux. Copyright © 1997 by Thomas Lux. Reprinted by permission of Houghton Mifflin Company. All rights reserved.

Cover Painting, *The Divide*, by David Haberman.

Cover Design by Joe Borsuk.

Manufactured in the United States of America
Published by Cleveland State University Poetry Center
Department of English
2121 Euclid Avenue
Cleveland, OH 44115-2214

ISBN: 1-880834-65-0
Library of Congress Catalog
Card Number: 2005920830

Ohio Arts Council
A STATE AGENCY
THAT SUPPORTS PUBLIC
PROGRAMS IN THE ARTS

In memory of my parents, John and Elizabeth,

and for Eileen, Mary Agnes, and Dan

CONTENTS

I

II

III

IV

V

A Small
Asymmetry

I

REDRESS

Something happened—*something* slipped from that dream
into the room,
and then a large, terrible insect
stung me on the face.

Had I injured her? Did I break something of hers
she loved?
Tearful, guilty, I remember walking
to where she was sleeping—but oh it was horrible—

the buzzing,
the large, black body with wings.
I didn't
defend myself—stung on the face

I told no one.
And what do I expect now, at sixty—
clarity? Ease? A body
free from scars?

Her room's gauzy light had always been
a comfort, its white lace curtains
lifting in a breeze—
she woke when I entered,

sat up, flushed, and showed me herself.
It *had* been a dream—she showed me herself
uninjured.
Have I been happy? Sure, I've been happy,

but afraid: that insect
is still here in the world—and this
I'm certain of: it *sought-me-out,*
it knew who I was.

LABYRINTH

They left her Aunt Mae's by midafternoon—up the steep Bronx hill,
then a right under the El, sun through the overhead tracks
a blinding strobe. *If ever I get that old*, she said,
just kill me. I will, he promised, a child's promise—just words

then and now: dutifully, he counts out her nineteen pills
into four small cups, lays out her diaper, helps her
up from the bed:
> *Who are you?*
> *Is this a house I'm in?*
> *How do I get to the outside?*

In the myth, Theseus had Ariadne to lead him out,
the Minotaur slain, the sacrifices over, but this
goes on and on, and in his heart he knows
he wants to do it—for himself: withhold some pills,
lead her in, not out, she
his gift—but then with no one but himself
to guide him back.

Like knives, she said, the pulsed light from the El so bothering her
she improvised a new route
home to Queens—smoking cigarettes, her left hand
draped out the window for turns, the other on the wheel, shifting,
her high heels on the pedals.
She was beautiful then, and wise,
and years younger than he is now.

ONCE MORE

In this my *(n+1)st* attempt at understanding just enough of Relativity
to grasp that time passes differently for me
if I'm accelerating relative to you, I've gotten this much straight:
light's speed is absolute—not space, not time—
making, theoretically, it possible for me to travel forward
to your future, you years older—by twenty, say, to my two—
maybe wiser, maybe philosophical by then
about my sudden rushing from this cottage to the beach
and vanishing, and not too pleased now to find me
young, eager, unlived,
out of place on your doorstep and expecting
what?…applause?…
for having pulled a stunt like that?

No. Better to be in your future in the future.
Better to be moving with you at any speed,
aging fast and more or less the same, you
refreshed by the sea and slightly burned,
smiling in from the side porch with your glass
of that expensive red you bought for dinner raised to me,
and me bringing the plates, the salad, the candles' light
absolutely perfect on your face.

NEIGHBOR

There in her backyard in the rain and crazier by the week,
my neighbor Joan is laying out the many *big*
blue pieces of her downstairs carpet on the grass,
"To clean them," she calls, holding up her Tide
and a long-handled brush, "just like the Persians in the villages!"

"They use *Tide?*" I ask, shocked stupid,
this never-dry-out, 5,000-pound, smell-bad disaster
pushed aside by an image of the orange box
set amid the rocks beside a stream in hills
near Hamadan.

And where the hell'd she find the strength of will
and just plain strength to rip it up and drag it out?
And yes, there's something I could say to her, something
I could do that might help
turn her from her hell-bent march to full-blown madness—

but I won't, I'll never be her friend: smart, short-fused,
aggressive, you give an inch she's calling,
leaving food, barging in and personal; slow it down
she's slamming doors, accusing, writing incoherent letters.
And I do not love her—except in theory.

So. I watch her sprinkle Tide, her white, loose underarm
shaking with the box.
I watch her spread it with the brush.
In the lightly falling rain I watch her
turning on the hose.

ONE-BEDROOM, FOUR FLOORS UP

Her life now unmade, the woman in slippers and red robe
blames years of comfort in her own home for spoiling her,
that's why, she tells herself, her heart's not in this,
but *she* is, so she might as well order the mirror
for the entrance hall, and the slender black pallas lamp for warmth.
But the lamp's gold paper shade is too dark in the catalog's
photograph, the mirror overpriced, and how, exactly,
will its pine frame look, rubbed with Napoleon Blue?

So if today she cannot make the call, if once more
that nameless rush of purpose has slipped from her as memory
slips from dreams, she can at least ride out the day,
just as, she thinks, the courtyard below
has ridden out the winter: the giant mulberry now thick with fruit,
a perch and feeder for the birds
nested in the ivy on the wall. It was the ivy and its sound
that drew her to the window, the ivy in bloom, its thick,
sweet scent drawing bees
in under the upturned palms of its leaves.
In the midday light the leaves are supple, a new
and brilliant green, and the bees brush them
with what seems to her a tenderness.

SHEILA'S AURAS

In my mother's talks with Christ he's dressed always
in a white gown and sandals, his light brown hair
long and flowing, his young, exposed heart
burning in his chest. That he's there to comfort her
after an "accident," or after a fall as the rich bruise
spreads beneath her skin, is OK with me, and OK too my lies

that 1) yes, I see him, just as 2) I claim to sort of see
my sister Sheila's auras, each of us, she says,
with a personal aurora borealis that I could learn to read—
like blood-work on the soul. Sheila worries
mine is dim, a queasy yellow. She says my mooning
for the world to mean more than I make it mean
is laughable, a kind of scientific/mythic schmutz
that locks me inside the field of light
buzzing at the surface of my eyes.

And yeah, OK, she's right—I'll never see my mother's Christ,
never see the auras. And the red fox that trotted up
out of the cemetery's ravine last week
and stood in the snow and stared at me, will never send a message
unless I make it—*my* hand and fingers
up inside *its* coat, *it* mouthing *my* thoughts, as if its being there
was only grist for my metaphoric mill, its mute
and indifferent *B* just an accident to serve my all consuming *A*,
as if that that stunning fox was just a mirror
to better see myself.

It left fresh tracks all week, looping,
impossible to follow. (Does it walk the same snow-holes,
coming and going?) Tonight, in her room,
Sheila combs my mother's hair. She tells her she can see
both Christ *and* His aura. My mother, smiling,
says of course, she never thought of it, her Christ

has always had a halo. And then they laugh, and Sheila
combs her hair: the antique comb,
Sheila's palm against my mother's head, their faces
beaming in the mirror.

II

SIGNS AND COSINES

I love *all* of it: algebra's unassuming and clever *x*
that you can add to anything, geometry's inscribed arcs and dropped
perpendiculars, trigonometry's tangent, the youthful
calculus, *Fuzzy Logic*, and these just the tip

of the certainty iceberg, the one that warms you
even in winter with its proofs—those elegant, no-going-back
(what's proved is proved) bones of its theorems, themselves
earnest, eager to work their symbolic asses
off for you—moving thought *and* mass: Viking *did*
reach Mars, and this 6-8-10 right-triangular planter,
the one for the lilac and penstemon, can
I know—the theorem meaning the same
in Greek, Korean, and American heads—be built
with my last two, straight, 12 ft. 4x4s.

What's straight in nobody's head is Pythagoras himself:
aristocrat, cult leader, perhaps
a native of Samos, the theorem probably his.
He was driven from Croton somewhere near 500 B.C.,
his followers years later victims of a purge
both bloody and thorough, and certain
to have struck them as cultural and arbitrary—
except those blows to their necks, which again mean the same
to Greek, Korean, and American heads.

ARTICLES OF EXPLORATION

That's one small step for man,
one giant leap for mankind.

—Neil Armstrong,
as he stepped onto the moon.

He singsonged it to himself as he studied the maps
of the Sea of Tranquility, he spoke it out loud in the shower—
That's one small step for a man,
one giant leap for mankind
but up there on the moon
he blew it, he got so caught up with getting down the ladder safely
he left out the rotten little *a*.

We knew what he meant, and he knew
we knew it, but he would have slapped his forehead
if he could have, and there was no going back up the ladder.

It's said he avoids interviews, doesn't attend celebrations
or go to reunions; in the midst of all that perfection
did something in him mean to screw it up? He'll never know.
Who was Deep Throat? Did Oswald act alone?

Years later when the first Viking landed on Mars,
nothing was said: the camera turned on, a door opened,
and the machine went to work. We could have given it speech,
we could have had it say—flawlessly—
That's one small step for a machine,
one giant leap for machinekind
but words, weighing too much, and with no human
to say them, just aren't worth it.

IN THE MEAN TIME

Deep as a heartbeat Bell Town's noon, its wired foothills
east of a southern plain and cooled
by a satellite's footprint, its late century air
thick with memory of imprecision, each sloppy chime
a roomful, each a fat margin on the crisp, nuclear,
thousandth of a millionth of a Greenwich second
stripped bare and broadcast click to lock,
locking the world. But Bell Town's Methodists

don't know—or do—their tower-on-the-hill's grandfather clock chorus
and twelve watery bongs
earnest beside the Catholic Angelus—
three sets of three, then 30 straight—the clever Episcopalians
last with songs we recognize and hum to. But *wrong*

the times say, that not-time's *off*, over
before it's rung, even the people are too wide, too slow,
their coming on now to the center
error prone, confused, their bells long in waves of blue on blue,
in heat, drifty, calling them
to calling them to calling them.

IN THE DESIGN REVIEW MEETING HE SAID

it *isn't* perfect, in fact I'll admit it's even a bit
fucked up here and there.
OK!—maybe more than just a bit,
more than just here and there, setting off a bang like that
definitely not my best. But look, we're stuck with it,

committed, and hey! time works, I like time,
and physics, chemistry, the *dynamics* of it all—
good, huh?
And photosynthesis, not bad—water, rain, the clouds, the sky
in general, day and night, rising moons—all that

I foresaw, that's mine. And color!, the senses, compassion,
sex!—sex is good, right?, they love sex! OK, perfect/
not-so-perfect. And yeah, death's a problem, all the killing,
maiming, eating,
all the just plain dying—blindsided, never saw it coming.

And their brains? Well, problems
far below the radar—missed them.
So OK, what do you want to do? Crucify me?
Funny.
Stop production? Close our doors? It *works*, they *won't* sue,

they don't *want* to sue—they blame themselves.
Yeah, I know, you want me outta here, but I'll be fine—
it will finally blow,
and there's nothing in this model that connects designer
to design.

HEY, HERE COMES GODOT

with a bag of bad news for the Information
Superhighway: *All the unknown still left on the streets*
he thunders, *will soon be known. You thought the supply
was endless, would be here forever to feed on,*

*but I tell you the bakers have stopped baking—
they're kneading out the last bit of resistance
from the last loaf, their fingers lost
in knowledge's floury dream of the unknown*

*risen to a golden brown certainty, its underside
crisp and blackened. "Eat this in memory of ignorance,"
they plan to say when they take it from the oven,
break it open, steaming, and butter it.*

So long, Godot says, packing up. *Forget those wafer words
sopping up sauce. What's here is that certain tomorrow's
rock-hard loaf, the last grist
for our wobbly, chiclet, piano-key teeth.*

IT WAS NOT A PIECE OF DRIFTWOOD AFTER ALL

but a turtle, its enormous shell part submerged, edges
flecked with yellow, its head raised just now to the light,
the air, bringing to whatever the shell protects
a form of peace or joy—who knows?

Looking past it all morning to the pond's
gel-like, solid muck of a surface one could walk on,
the wood's tall light shimmering in the few clear patches
still able to ripple in the breeze, I worked again

my old questions: how to be a part of that,
what to *do* with it.
I had just sealed my mouth to its filthy, lipless mouth
in a fury, to suck it in, to suck from it every cold life

and decomposing death it held,
every grace, every wide-eyed horror—fish, rotting bird, snake—
nothing not tasted, faced, the molecules of every stench
passed through me, eaten—

when the turtle raised its head.
I can't not watch the living head: an awareness
unaware of being watched, it just now arched its neck, the movement
the movement of my thumb, a kind of speech

I should but don't know.
That life knows nothing of our bright technology,
our models for the stars,
for what's beyond them.

It drifts, at last dips its head, rolls a bit
and disappears. Wanting nothing from me, it meant nothing to it
that I watched; sure that we're unwatched,
I could not look away.

BIRDING

So OK, if to have this kind of soul
requires awareness of it, maybe the soul itself
the awareness, which is what, anyway?—a chemical state
of a chunk of brain, some voltages, a physical pattern,
an *idea*?—then does its leaving us at death just mean

us ceasing to think it? That loss, though,
the loss of something real, that state of brain as real
as the real sparrow the real jay in my gutter
is holding up in its beak
as if to examine again the sparrow's bloody neck,

maybe to judge again if the sparrow's soul
has yet left *it*, the jay's discontent an engine
forcing it to force the sparrow back down
into the gutter, back to its driving its sleek, black, stiletto beak
into the sparrow's neck.

But from down here little is clear: I can't see enough through time
to grasp the whole design: their souls, the initial meeting of the two—
but the rapid gutter-tinny hammering of the jay's beak,
the goddamn jay again
holding the sparrow up, the sparrow's head again lolling,

wings a few times jerky-flapping, the sparrow
not yet soulless, maybe even thinking—*all that* I get,
and the jay and the jay's soul at one in a seamless one
with its soul-neighborhood, soul-clan, soul-nation,
its physiologic built-in built-ins humming, the *information*

and *cohesion* of it all, the whole bird-gutter thing ancient,
balanced, complete, the jay owning its particular killer beak
but not the idea of its beak—that soul, all that I get,
which I know is good, natural, and unlike me down here
stuck with both—destructiveness *and* the idea of it—

down here where there's a gap, a problem, in fact it's said
a bottomless abyss that's *our* responsibility—
which it is, yes, the jay grinding to bits in a tinny gutter a sparrow
the world's greatest piece of cake next to this Grand Canyon
of a soul-gulf we've supposedly made and keep

calling into, keep flashing light down into in search
of *something* back, a reflection, an echo,
some awareness that says I'm here you're there, *something*
besides what's coming back right now, that damn jay's hammering
stopped, its glare down at me and harsh laugh-calling

enough for me to want to kill it, to try to stop it,
dislodge-disconnect it from the dopey sparrow, pure
brainless anarchy these little rocks I'm throwing, almost
breaking a window, His Oneness the Jay laughing, happy,
content because expecting *nothing*

other than what is, expecting nothing more today or less
than to kill this sparrow, *that* jay holding up again the sparrow
in its beak, lifting easily with it on the air
and away—the No-Soul-Gap Jay—*that* jay with no thought ever
for a better world.

III

TWO DREAMS

The Nazis in the first dream were ascendant again
in Europe: the same black uniforms
returned to our streets, the same efficiency to our lives.
Only me and some woman were worried.

And in the second, the wedding dream, we arrived in the rain—
singly and in pairs—to a cathedral in Paris:
delighted with our grown-up selves after fifty years apart,
we hugged, yelled, and kissed. Eleanor was still young,

so she and that group of fools, the ones with broken hearts,
were given parts to play in a drama
for the altar. The rest of us—at the sound of a trumpet—
rushed through the pews looking for prizes.

She married a man none of us knew.
The wedding party—bride and groom, maid-of-honor and best-man,
bridesmaids and ushers—smiled from the altar as the red drapes
were quickly closed; when opened, they all had vanished.

We left to streetlights and a city shining with rain.
I know dreams act alone, but here, blocking both ends of the long,
narrow Rue Foucault, smacking their bats in their palms—
the Nazis were waiting.

IMAGES

Red Riding Hood is having a bad dream—Grandma's house
a hut of boards and corrugated tin, its front door
a hollow closet door, and the forest around it has gathered itself
and stares at the house like an animal, its alert, implacable mind
made up.

> *Three electron guns—called the red, blue, and green guns—*
> *are mounted in the narrow neck of a large electron tube.*
> *The guns generate three electron beams, each beam*
> *scanned across over five hundred horizontal lines*
> *on the face of the tube, one line at a time, top to bottom,*
> *first the even numbered, then the odd numbered lines.*

Swinging her legs from the sagging bed, Red Riding Hood's foot
lands in an image of the window
cast by the moon on the floor. Lines so simple,
she reaches into the light with an image of a bird, flying.

> *As the beams scan each line, they strike thousands of sets*
> *of three phosphor dots—red, blue, and green—*
> *placed along the line. A shadow mask guides each beam*
> *so that the proper beam strikes the proper colored dot*
> *in each set. The intensity of the light emitted by a dot*
> *depends on the intensity of its beam at the moment*
> *the dot is struck by the beam as the beam scans past.*

Encouraged by her bird, Little Hood tries others—a dog, barking,
a spider on the pane. But whatever she makes and withdraws,
the moon waits with the window's image, so at last
she lies down on the floor in the moon's window.

> *The beams, dots, and light from the scans*
> *form a sequence of sixty interlaced pictures each second.*

Through the eye's persistence, the pictures appear to a viewer
as an image both moving and real.

It was in the news from South Africa—years ago—
a video crew recorded a crowd's murder of a child,
nine or ten years old, the daughter of an informer or policeman.
When she answered her door they struck her with knives
and small hatchets. You could see her face when she realized her fate.
She took the first blows and then ran down a path and fell
with her arms oddly raised. And after she fell,
her body took blows as meat takes blows, and with each blow
her hands bobbed in a graceful, limp way.
As she died, her fingers slowly opened.

The electrical video signal that contains the image
continuously changes the intensity of each electron beam
in order to produce the image in light.
Once the beams and dots transform the image into light,
it is said to have become a real image.
The viewer sees the real image by changing the light
back to electrical signals understood by the brain.

As Red Riding Hood lay on the floor, the woodsman and wolf
pounded on the door. *The violence of the sun,* the moon told her,
warms me and gives me form.
Looking down at herself, Red Riding Hood saw the image
of the window; as the door flew open she stood up
and with the help of the moon stepped through
for a second time.

BY ANY OTHER NAME

No, not gen-mmh-mmh, no one
wants talk of that again in Europe.
Better the euphemism, and better
that inefficient, poor-man's system
to help twist the name: make them
your enemy's problem, like wounded, like a city's homeless
squared—few bullets wasted,
lost soldier-hours digging holes reduced, logistics
up and running: just fear (already there)
and roads (already there),
just kill two hundred here two hundred there
to raise to white-hot pitch the first
and get them moving on the second.

To *cleanse* means to purify,
absolve of sin, the word's scent
the scent of laundry
snapping on the line, a soaped-up washcloth of a word
next to godliness.

And e*thnic*—the sound of baklava and tortellini,
the Festival and Grandma's broken English—

the words in combination cleansed themselves,
sliding through the mind and dragging with them nothing
of the *cide* in mmh-mmh-mmh.

The big mistake was putting some of them on trains, giving us
that long-lensed image—

> *rippling heat against the rising ties*
> *the curving rails and flattened onto cars*
> *the siding's booted guards' insignias and standing armed*
> *apart the separate hands the windows*

kerchiefed at the eyes the mouths
below the power lines compressed above
the shriek the whistle
you can hear the you can see the

like a hook in bone, dragging
from its plain-sight hiding place in bottom mud,
up through names designed like camouflage,
a giant catfish by the mouth.

There are different ways to skin a cat
because to skin a cat is hard.
My friend in Alabama nails them belly down
through the head
to a flat board, then makes a cut from cheek to cheek
to get a grip with pliers, the skin
torn off in strips.
Just a fish, she says—
relax.

SYMBOLIC

Someone tore down my neighbors' flag last night,
a stars and stripes with rainbow stripes
flown by two men, who also fly Old Glory.
Someone tore it down, then, two streets over,
doused the flag with gasoline and burned it.

Not a hate crime the police said, but hate it was,
teenage hate, some boys—it had to be boys,
maybe a girlfriend along to impress—but boys
in search of ground to stand on, maybe one of them
gay himself and terrified, but both—there had to be two—
doused the flag with gasoline and burned it.

Did they plan it? Were they drunk? Did they bring the gas,
or did one of them—the kid by himself, eager
to impress his friend's girlfriend—did he go home afterward
and get the can, the furled flag still whole
in the back seat, still able to rebuke them?
He did. This not-so-bad kid got his can of mower gas, then
doused the flag with gasoline and burned it.

My neighbors say they'll never fly their flags again. Theirs
is a small Craftsman house with a wide,
wrap-around porch, different, but also like the others—
just a house, just two men in love, maybe in the sixties
only children, maybe infants, maybe still unborn that June day
we marched in protest—for peace and love—and from his pack,
and to our cheers, someone took a stars and stripes,
doused the flag with gasoline and burned it.

RELATIVITY

I *think* I have—certainty by now a mockery
with the great Newton overthrown,
and the rumor of a *d* squared in Pythagoras's triangle—
gotten rid of the smell of cat piss
in my entrance foyer

by tearing out the molding, gouging out
the wood beneath, applying urethane so thick
it cracks, the gap caulked shut, the cat
dead, or so I like to believe, its bladder by now
decomposed, the neural patterns that drove it

to the east corner of the foyer perhaps not gone
from the earth, but gone from that miserable cat's
misuse of them, and gone too from the lives
of the real culprits—the prior tenants,
sweet Carrie and Doctor Rob—

who didn't have the fortitude to train poor Fluffy—
yes, *Fluffy*—who didn't have the nose
for it either and must have grown to love
their foul foyer, that space that each morning
after showers and each evening after work

said to them maybe Mommy or maybe Daddy or maybe
dinner or cozy or even Home Sweet Home,
but said to me that first night with a certainty
surpassing even Einstein's—Me! Mine!
Trespasser! Filth! Flea! Flee!

THE LARGE ANT THAT WAS WANDERING

the far end of this bench, maybe the same ant as yesterday,
maybe here since dawn, assigned
since childhood, this bench its life's work of checking out a twig,
a drop of water, what fell here overnight,
the ant that just now turned and headed toward my foot—for it
I slapped the bench and drove it nuts.

I could kill it.
I've killed hundreds, thousands like it—
bam! dead! Like the many-legged, long-legged,
thread-legged
spidery-like bug with the little gray-brown button body
I just killed or maimed,
harmless, frightening things, this one walking on my arm—
swept it off, broke some legs, who knows?—
impossible to find down there.

What is *wrong* with me? Who gives a damn about a bug,
alive one moment dead the next?
That fast, that simple, like drawing one thin line
across another.
But that's it, Moira, isn't it? That moment, the edge,
the crossing, the irreversibility,
you alive, one instant one thing—

and that's worth putting in my skin, Moira,
repeatedly, that edge, to feel
the idea in it, to cross
and cross that line until it's raw,
the idea numb.
Moira, to remember you, to symbolize this world,
I've crushed the ant.

SOLSTICE

My neighbor's attic light is on again. It happens
maybe twice a year: a bare bulb hanging
from a cord, the stark light
reflected off the rafters' silvered insulation
giving to my upstairs hall an eerie glow—where I pace,
awake again at three in pain.

Looked at from below, the window
shows only insulation, rafters, and the bulb—
a rough, mechanical intelligence to which I give
tonight the burden of my vanity and rage, my jealousies,
greed, my need to win—the list
endless—my heart dismayed, eager
to be a different heart.

At the roof's peak the moon is stuck to the sky
like a small bright button, reflected light
spread so thin over this world
it's wan, pathetic, diminished by the window.

It takes the twisted shadows of the bare trees—sharp
and shot across the lawns—to finally brighten everything,
the moon's light seeming now pervasive,
deep. My heart will never change,
and I cannot have a different heart. And never
do I tell my neighbors their light is on—it's on for days,
then one night it's off.

LAND'S HOUSE

In the walls of the land's house the rodents are dying.
To escape their sound, their smell,
I've stretched myself out here in the exact center of the land's carpet,
here with the scraps of food, the grease, the ants,
and worse—the bacteria swarming, and the heads,
antennas, thousands of legs ready to be born.

And I can see from here the land's ceiling is cracked,
that yellow stain a sign of worse to come.
And the basement?—don't ask—I can smell it,
half filled with water half the time, the large spiders…

Please come home.
The work involved, the expense—it's far more than I bargained for,
I'm not smart enough to handle it alone.
Please—come here and save me from this runaway sorrow
that's never quite worked out.

In me in images—the government brochure and its stories.
The laughing printed family at the kitchen table,
the printed father handsomely dressed in slacks, white shirt,
striped tie—
in him I'm printed laughing in images with the printed mother,
the printed child.
But where is my dinner in the land's house?
And why the land's sky now purple-black,
the wind now slamming the wind chime into itself—
a violent metallic banging of the air's knife?
And the courage to stand here facing into that wind?—where did we
    get it?
From an anarchy bred into us?
From a knowledge that the worst is suffering
and that we were and were not built to withstand it?

From fury at a design
even we can imagine improving on?
How, in us, exactly, was it ever worked out
that we could stand here like this in the rain, like the hero in that movie
standing in the rain on the roof of his car,
a bad, bad day,
his face slammed at the sky?

The land's night now peaceful, the brochure at dinner,
its cups, glasses, plates,
all its silverware in use,
and it makes me joyful to have been asked in here with them,
the printed guest in his casual,
yellow printed shirt, in here where I can see now that this,
the land's house,
isn't more than I bargained for, the leaks fixable,
the smells airable.

And they're proud of me—this family—proud of my bravery,
they show me their small, brown dog
who looks to me like it lives in the land's walls,
a rodent of a dog,
smells like it, those claws and teeth—
a ferret of a dog—and why it lives,
and why it keeps wanting to live
is beyond me.
And when I tell them their dog is a rat dying in their walls,
when I reveal to them they've a daughter—a runaway named Sorrow—
who's bitter and sick,
and who's living in the walls of their house,
this family who asked me to dinner has asked me to leave—
ungrateful, betrayed they said

when they left for their attic where they—
or something—is banging around.

Sorrow come out now, through the outlets, the fixtures,
like smoke,
into the safety of the land's house.
What happened hasn't undone you—
your stories and startle.
Let's bring them down now, Sorrow,
from their attic, where I think they're lonely.
Sorrow let's hug them, feed them,
let's bathe them, Sorrow, and put them to bed.

IV

PHYSICAL

It's *nothing*, he says, a small asymmetry, we'll check it out
when you get back. The worst—it's cancer; the best—
it's just you.
Is he *crazy*? When I get *back*? The million dollar rented beach house
turned to stomach acid? *Do—it—now*! I shout,

shaking him, let's check it out *yesterday*, this town bursting
with urologists just sitting on their hands—
where they rest them when they're idle.
Friends, have physicals in Fall, with nothing planned.

A small asymmetry. A bad sign for one who's been symmetric
all his life—write with the right, throw with the left,
when praised, quick to name a fault.
That's *balance*, he says, not symmetry, and on his pad
he draws a circle. Prostate—the size of a walnut,

pale, firm, partly muscle partly gland, a fist
at the base of the urethra, and *yours*, he says, is slightly
asymmetric—on his circle he draws a bulge
from 12 to 3. You're *fine*! It's *nothing*! *Relax*!

And what *would* I have him do? Cry out, *Oh, no!*
when he felt me? And he's right, it *is* balance we're after,
not symmetry, not that static, sentimental same-old same-old
across a boundary, one side unable to give
or teach anything to the other, our deep dislike of symmetry
the reason we marry opposites, not clones, the reason one foot
is always larger than the other, one heart, one lopsided stomach,
the reason first there's *A*, then *B*, the reason one-fourth of my walnut—
from 12 to 3—struck out on its own and bulged
into asymmetry. So…OK… I'll go. It *is* nothing.

I'll put on my Ray-Ban Cats, rub on my #20 Bain de Soleil.

I'll put on my aqua Speedo trunks and my black Rockport thongs.
I'll put on my Spiegel rugby shirt, and my Yankees baseball hat.
I'll carry my red aluminum beach chair and reed mat
under my left arm, and my all-cotton towel and rainbow umbrella

under my right. I'll carry my cooler bag and my book bag
over opposite shoulders, and carefully, it being just myself,
I'll walk my newly strange asymmetric body—feeling now
like a threat—down to the sea.

THE *SIG* IN *FLEX-SIG*

is for the sigmoid colon, and *flex* for flexible
since what they slip inside you is not—thank God—
a rod. And if you decline the Demerol-Versed mix
you get to watch it on the monitor, although
for this you pay
at and with the bends, meaning

both what they go around and what you do
when they go around them (or do more of—your knees
already at your chest), as unimaginative a name for pain
as fly is for a fly, or orange for an orange,
but pain well worth it: lit up (the clarity
amazing, the color bright, the picture big) it's a *friendly*

part of you, working…well…its head off, and *not*
what you'd think: well-veined, smooth,
bright and shiny, the racing scope with images a spelunker
would die for, that word the word of the day,
why you're there, picking up the tone, smiling
at the jokes, trying to think of one yourself

(as if they hadn't heard them all), listening
for their subtle change in focus, their loss of playfulness,
hoping not to see what you had come in fear to see—
or not—your age and history closing in,
and you still clearheaded, presumably still able
to drive yourself home.

LACKAWANNA

The last billet to be rolled in America is in the furnace,
and Dick Tracy is standing by.
The world has been made safe for democracy,
and the world is better off for LaGuardia
having read the funnies to the kids over the radio.
Tracy is standing by with memories of a Fox Trot America
two-by-two, and the GIs triumphantly home
because it was we who had won the war.

As the billet is pushed from the furnace
Tracy mounts the control pulpit. In the glowing heat
he once again sees the dietary pie-charts of America—
the dairy and grain, the fresh meat and vegetables.
He can smell the java, and the ham and the eggs
and the once-over-easy
as he sets up to roll the last billet to be rolled in America.

Tracy knows he must roll a tongue—
a tongue to lick the immigrants' dust from the mill floor,
a tongue to guide the liquid steel from the open throats
of the blacks, to thrill at the salt in the blood,
a steel tongue for a steel rage,
a ribbon of steel to lick wounds.

Tracy's eyes glow red, they send red down through his arms,
red into red hands to grip steel.
But in the first pass in the roughing stand the billet misforms,
and Tracy hears the crystallized scream
of the earth: crushed, sintered, flowing and held down
for the white hot obscenity of steel breaking steel.

Tess is gone. B.O. Plenty is gone.
The blast furnaces are rubble at his feet

and Tracy is now wild in the pulpit.
He is beginning to sob, and the teardrops and sweat
leap comic-strip-style
from his squared-off face.
He is calling on his little, obsolete wrist-radio
for an understanding of the birthing of a tongue:
he is calling Kennedy and King,
he is calling up the old neighborhoods,
he is calling Iwo Jima,
he is calling up every word that has ever screeched
from his radio's little speaker.

Outside the mill, the people are standing in lines.
From the screens of their radio-videos
the image of Tracy rides to their eyes: Tracy's not selling steel,
he's not selling games, and he sure as hell's not selling jobs:
the billet is cobbled in the finishing stands
and Tracy is slumped in the pulpit.

Dick Tracy we lift you in hands bruised in the mill,
touch you to our wounds.
Tracy in hard hat and mackinaw, eased back to his comic-strip page.
Tracy at sixty just fiction, and standing in line:

> Braddock, Lackawanna,
> Youngstown, Aliquippa,
> Lorain, Iron Mountain, Birmingham,
> Cleveland, Bucks County, Gadsden,
> Provo, Hibbing, Johnstown, Bethlehem,
> Pittsburgh, Wheeling, Portage,
> Brackenridge, Duluth,
> Ashland...

AT THE ATM IN GOCEK

That the key-pad has no letters and I've memorized my PIN
as a word is nothing
next to last night's airport van ride through the mountains,
but still—where exactly did I press?!

And now the young Turkish cop who's watching from the door
wants to help. Bored maybe, and dressed
tourist-friendly: ordinary dark blue pants, light blue
short-sleeve shirt open at the neck, no hat, no badge,

no straps or belt of stuff—just a radio and gun—
but I'm afraid of him, afraid that if I guess wrong and screw this up
he'll grab me, drag me out of line—
even though there is no line.

English he says in English, walking over, and hits the key
to do the deal in English. (How did he know?
My two friends in wicker cowboy hats?)
No letters, I say, pointing, but he doesn't understand, my face

now hot with criminality: we all should *know* our PINs,
and I've no pen to write an *A*, a *B*, a question mark,
it doesn't even cross my mind, this guilt—
where does it come from?—freezing me,

the yellow ATM a road I'd like right now to click
my sandals on and go back home. *ENTER!* he says
a little forcefully, but then we're at the *PIN!*—
and this guy's looking more and more to me

like that prison guard in *Midnight Express*, like the officer
in that scene in *Lawrence of Arabia* where they break him,
and maybe—why not?—he's still pissed at Europe's old plan
to divvy up the Sick Man of Europe,

and just exactly *what* does he think of the Kurds, the Armenians,
the Greeks, the West, the East, Islam, the Fundamentalists, democracy,
the army—this guy's *face* that strange face
in Byzantine mosaics, the face of all that Sultan-Harem stuff

that scared me as a kid—I'll *never* get this PIN—
he'll draw his gun, shoot me, drag me off to prison—
NO LETTERS! I say, smiling,
almost mouthing it, then hit *CANCEL* and grab my card.

He shrugs, walks off—doesn't give a damn.
And it will take me all day to figure out the letters start at 2,
and there's no Q in the sequence—
my PIN in Turkey

> *bits-of-history, scraps-of-facts,*
> *just-passing-through,*
> *can't-speak-a-word, haven't-got-a-clue,*
> *scary-Byzantine-Sultan-Harem-stuff.*

HEADS

I was glad my parents'
heads were normal-size.
　　　　　　—Thomas Lux

Small heads atop the otherwise normal people
in his hometown—not on everyone,
but on enough of them for him to undergo some tests
on his own head. I read that in a good poem
by a good poet, his heads in the poem metaphorical,

but maybe not invented: at six
he could have thought he really saw small heads,
the poem, its metaphor, allowing for that,
between invention and truth they could, as we say, care less.
But I on this gray morning care more,

my own head in the mirror *large*
and seeming—as I look—to get larger. No, not booze, not drugs,
and no, not metaphor. Just a bigger looking head,
thicker, broadened overnight by an inch, lengthened
by two, my torso the same, my head *large*,

but large with what? No fat on it anywhere, no chins, my nose
not yet given up the ghost and spread. Maybe
water. Or maybe arthritis of the brain,
that stiffening behind the eyes and ears
that swells the head and shrinks the world,

brought on by too much talk, too much conviction,
and no known cure. Just meditation
to prevent the onset of a final, dull,
enormous knowledge of the world
called *topple-over-head*, the cranial cavity shrunk

to the size of a baseball, the head all bone and *large*,
a lot like what I'm looking at right now, that poet's town
maybe sitting near a large-head sanitarium—one offering
a cure—but on no map, at no place
except inside his budding-poet child's head.

TRUST ME

—*for Anne*

I—have—had-it! Let the fucking house fall down around me.
Let the next big wind—forecast for this afternoon—
knock completely flat all the unstaked phlox and cosmos
swaying in the front bed. Fuck the clogged gutters and leaking roof
no roofer calls back about, and the five *viburnum tomentosum*
I've no time to buy and plant—*fuck* those five—
and fuck too all the email needing answers.
Fuck the ants in my kitchen. And the sun-filled, deep-blue sky?—
fuck that for no good reason. And *Oh, yes*—
double fuck the unused treadmill in my basement.

No, I said to her last night at Angelo's, *I haven't done
what I was sent to do* (though no one and nothing, I believe,
has sent me). *But no, this specific DNA
feels he hasn't done it—not
enough ability, determination, courage—whatever.
And besides* (I said into that knowing look of hers I hate),
*what we finally do is what we're sent to do.
Look at me, I'm 65!—my manual
never having had a mission under "mission" in the index.*

We drank the wine, ate the food, I paid the bill with a card
taken from that life whose blue-sky sun-lit house has in it
among the ants and me a teenage son
I'm pushing through a door we've both been leaning on
for years: *You'll do fine,* I tell him—
*just try things, do them, it may be hard,
give it time, it'll work—trust me.*

LICENSE

1.

You hit a cone you're done, so *forget*
the rear-view mirror. You've got to twist your body,
put your right hand
back behind the seat—*you've got to do it!*—
and look back through the rear window even if
sitting there beside you the examiner's a she—
she won't think you're leaning in to kiss her.
You've got to do it!

I know him—he won't do it.

2.

And yeah, of course she *is* a she and young and yes
he's backing up into that maze of cones
looking in the mirror.
Look back!
You *need* this badge—*Do-it! Do-it! Do-it!*
Your facial hair dark, thick,
but hair right now is not enough—*Do-it!*—
it's not too late—look back—
put your arm behind her seat!

3.

There must be, up there, a Driving God
because he's turning now, reaching back, twisting, looking back
through the window,
backing toward me, luminous,
his snaked, brake-lit passage through the cones enough to damage
his and two parked cars but leaving

five sweet orange cones—
I kiss them kiss them—
standing.

4.
He's done it—the rest was cake.
Laminated mug shot serious, choosing
to keep his eyes and heart,
he's grinning from the driver's window, waving,
waving from the train, the jet-way, waving
from the ship, he's beaming waving, looking back
twisting back
waving, waving.

WAITING FOR THE MUSE IN LAKE VIEW CEMETERY

These two young shirtless guys in cutoffs don't fit here,
they're walking too fast—straight at me—they don't look
at the three-foot lion sitting on Baby O'Donnell's grave, nor at the
    Hermes
reaching for the knocker on the door to Hades. No, these guys

don't look at shit, unless you count me,
their black t-shirts, leather pants and shaved heads
badly out of place next to the mini-Parthenon mausoleum
and the threadleaf maples, and no way am I some Eurydice

and these two the Orpheus Brothers with rescue
on their minds. And I'm thinking now how *stupid* can you get
to wander an empty, hilly, heavily wooded cemetery alone,
and just where are the grasscutters when you need them, and why

all this Greek myth stuff when I'm dealing with two guys
in military jackets and those black gloves with the stiff,
funnel-shaped wrist covers, two maniacs
who have now lowered the tinted visors on their helmets

and are revving their Harleys as they weave toward me, crushing
the pachysandra, blowing kisses, calling, "We've got something
    fooor you"—
for *me!* who came here *humble*, with a bowed head,
a petitioner to the Muse for *anything*—a fragment of a voice

with a little authority, a feeling, a fragment of an idea,
who wanted only...well...OK...
who maybe lied about the Hermes and the lion,
and yeah, the two guys were the grasscutters, and no,

they didn't come near me, but I lied only because I thought
I was supposed to, that to lie put me on the road to truth,
guided there by Herself, a Greek woman in a white robe
and not two lousy bikers who have now, by the way,

ridden pretty far off, and who, unlike Orpheus,
won't look back, despite my yelling after them, their red
enameled gas tanks flashing in the sun, their exhausts
now just sweet, fading, throaty rumbles.

THE DOMESTIC ANIMAL'S INSERTION

I said It feels like a loss of emotional memory,
maybe a touch of dementia.
She said You don't *have*
an emotional memory—
you *respond* with emotions.

I said I'm aging, experiencing
a cooling of passion—like what happens to cats.
She said You're depressed,
take a pill, I know the name
of someone to talk to.

I said It might be a slight calcification or blockage of something
up in my brain, or maybe
a natural slowing—like what happens to cats.
She said Stop whining, do aerobics—
what's with the cats?

I said Without those inspired, voice-making rushes,
without those impassioned illogical leaps I'm just here in my head
twisting talk,
nailing up language like wallboard,
hanging up prints.

She said Forget it, you—I said Wait. What I'm after is sound
as graceful as sea grass, for meaning as open
as brush strokes, for a syntax—She said Yeah, well,
I'm as calm as a joke
swept through with as old as my radio's on

and no coffee today.
I said What?—She said Look,
you won't find what you want fracturing sense,

mooning for sound. Voice
is shaped by your life.

I said Yes well OK I'm—She said I sing to you in the dark,
I usher you daily between this world
and that other world whose source is me.
I said Yes I—She said Don't ignore my appearance
in change—

look up. There's longing forever,
for all of us,
there are losses and fear.
She said And please—cats grow wise, or don't matter:
don't fuck with me please with the cats.

THE READING

No matter how elaborate my preparations, no matter what
insights I have, what promises I make, when I reach
this moment when everything depends upon breath—

I'm breathless. I've even tried the Anne Guzzardi
Anti-Anxiety Method of balancing on one foot, with that foot's toes
bent under, its brilliant disorientation

designed to loosen the mind's claustrophobic, heart-pounding
death-grip on the lungs
and turn it to the fine motor skills, to the generation of those delicate,

precise, almost sweet nerve impulses we need
to keep from falling over, but a shift which for me—
today and every day—

fails, forcing me to read
in gasps, crackles, out at the end of my pulmonary tether
in squeaks, my struggle ancient, now public and squarely

my fault: no excusing genetics, nothing congenital,
just the big-self setting the small-self adrift again
in its leaking boat—wee voice of the body,

hands, hair, voice of longing, voice of woe,
voice of the great idea—
naked voice drowning in air.

HAVING DONE ALL THE SHOPPING
I CAME FOR

Yesterday I read perfectly the words in the first line,
with tenacity, exerting over them and the world
a power of mind that will keep me in the world.
But by the end of the second line I had forgotten
the first line's meaning, and going back
forgot the second's.

And now having done all the shopping I came for,
why am I *here* standing at Bed Bath & Beyond's ceiling-high display
of kitchen utensils? Why so *calm*,
so at ease just staring, thoughtless, at a mountain
of spoons and graters?

But here's a winged corkscrew I need, something
six months ago—bolted tight into life—
I would have rushed past and left behind.

But why so at *peace*, why so calm in a blankness
that feels like a clock has stopped?
And now here's a digital counter that counts up
as well as down, what I've needed for over a year
to time the reading of poems.

But why so at *peace*, why so calm in a blankness
that feels like a clock has stopped?
Why so centered in my green StratoJac
down jacket, puffed and powerful
like the Michelin Man, and happy to have in his basket
a corkscrew and counter?

WITH MY BACK TURNED TO ITS QUESTION

If it breaks, it doesn't matter.
If it didn't come back this Spring, forget it, get another one,
something yellow, small passions of bloom you wished
would sweep you one more time.

The swollen river carried off cattle, homes,
so many lives lost, so many more lives to come
and you are far from that river—nothing you can do,
forget it.
The millions of mouths beneath these lawns? The longing for wings
beating above the canopy?
Once upon a time there was contact, but they were hoping
we were God.

In my flying dream I'm dressed in a white gown like Christ,
my outstretched arms rigid wings,
my soaring high over hundreds of thousands of small suburban houses
a blessing, the *height* and exposure miraculous.
But looking down I'm given to feel I will live forever—
horrible the claustrophobia,
never to be released.

There is a kind of falling apart of hope that feels like the sound of tires
on a gravel drive in August,
like the start of a breathless, heart-pounding freedom
responsibility mutes, transforms, makes one forget—
or afraid—to use.
What's to be known by me in this span of time
I think I know.

My body was the first to tell me I would live forever.
My parents took it up, my teachers, I took it up,
in the face of all that was in the world,

the world took it up.
Then release—the idea—was skipped like a flat stone
over the pond of my life, a small *slip-zip*
at each touch to my thought, my present hardly disturbed.
When at last it slowed it cut in,
tumbled and fell.
I thought it was something else, I had always planned to use it,
but its tumbling down *was* my life.

My mother loved lilacs and taught us lilacs and wild roses.
I built her a small pond in the back, a shallow, oval hole
really, a child's idea of a pond,
stagnant, at last leaky, a cement-filled depression they knew
would fail—
but they let me do it, let me wreck their yard,
watching from the window.
I mourned her when she died long before she died;
when she finally died I said little, felt little, having myself
forgotten our lives together.

The single principle that invents time, giving it sweetness
and shape, is the principle of collapse, breakage, repetition—
again and again the snow comes.
Cycles, and all the talk of the rhythm of cycles,
a weariness: repetition, knowledge—
engines dragging me forward, beneath them my tongue
stuck to a frigid slab of black steel, a featureless, implacable block
that without collapse, breakage, repetition,
is time whole,
unmoving, undifferentiated.

My father died long before that.
They told us to call him back if he slipped into a coma,

so *Jack! Jack!* we yelled.
I am a fish at the bottom of a pond, he said to us
in a moment of clarity, *The sides are slippery-slimy, green-slimy—*
when you call to me I must struggle up but I slip
and slide back, I struggle up and slide back—it's horrible
to struggle like that—please don't call me back.
We never saw him again.

The principle of collapse a design so at odds with my ambition,
with my hopes and longing—
should I change what I am to suit it? Should I come to believe that I am
what I'm not to be happy?
Once upon a time there were wings above the canopy—
I *hear* that stone skipping the surface, slicing in
and tumbling.
It's falling down to him, falling to her,
my son calling to me, that stone only a stone,
tumbling, with no choice in this or anything.
Once upon a time in a story I woke to myself
whole and complete as an answer—dislodged from its question—
with my back turned to its question.
In that story my hands, not wings, are the load-bearing characters.

FLYAWAY

I must get home—our house might have sold,
or the one we're bidding on may need
a counteroffer. Or the lawyer
handling the agreement for the land
might have called. How

irresponsible—
to sit here in this hot sun,
motionless,
so that the jet-black dragonfly that landed
on my knee
will not fly off. Oblivious

of these eyes,
this mind, it relaxed its legs
in three
distinct
stages,
then lowered its black shimmering body
to my skin.

I'll never see this again, never succeed
in doing anything with it.
And tonight in the house that might have sold
I'll fail—and may not even try—
to describe to you how its black lace wings
opened   and closed
once   each second.

NOTES

"The Domestic Animal's Insertion": The title of this poem
alludes to W.B. Yeats's poem, "The Circus Animals' Desertion."

IMAGINATION SERIES

#1. Holbrook, Sara. *Chicks Up Front*. ISBN 1-880834-39-1 (paper), 64 pp., $9.00.

#2. Vigil, Anthony. *The Obsidian Ranfla*. ISBN 1-880834-43-X (paper), 88 pp., $12.00.

#3. Seibles, Tim. *Hammerlock*. ISBN 1-880834-45-6 (paper), 120 pp., $14.00.

#4. Andrews, Nin. *The Book of Orgasms*. ISBN 1-880834-48-0 (paper), 80 pp., $14.00.

#5. Gonzalez, Gaspar Pedro. *The Dry Season: Qu'anjob'al Maya Poems*. ISBN 1-880834-53-7 (paper), 112 pp., $14.00.

#6. Michaux, Henri. *Someone Wants to Steal My Name*. Nin Andrews, ed. ISBN 1-880834-56-1 (paper), 120 pp., $14.00.

#7. Seibles, Tim. *Buffalo Head Solos*. ISBN 1-880834-63-4 (paper), $16.00; 1-880834-64-2 (cloth), $25.00, 152 pp.

#8. Donoghue, John. *A Small Asymmetry*. ISBN 1-880834-65-0 (paper), 80 pp., $14.00.

#9 Kovacik, Karen. *Metropolis Burning*. ISBN 1-880834-66-9 (paper), 80 pp., $14.00.

The Cleveland State University Poetry Center is the publisher of 145 collections of contemporary poetry since 1971.

To place a book order, call 1-888-278-6473 toll free (216-687-3986 locally). Fax: 216-687-3986.
E-mail: poetrycenter@csuohio.edu.
Website: www.csuohio.edu/poetrycenter.
Titles also available on amazon.com.

Cleveland State University Poetry Center
Department of English
2121 Euclid Avenue
Cleveland OH 44115-2214